Enter & Win The Green Card Lottery

To order additional copies, please contact us.
BookSurge, LLC
www.booksurge.com
1-866-308-6235
orders@booksurge.com

Enter & Win The Green Card Lottery

Clinton Jones

2005

Enter & Win The Green Card Lottery

Cover Illustration

Entitled: *"Be Patriotic" sign your country's pledge to save the food.* The work was undertaken by popular magazine illiustrator of the day—Paul Stahr, done in Gouache on paper it is to be found at the *Herbert Hoover Library, National Archives and Records Administration*

Designed to instill patriotism, confidence, and a positive outlook, War Posters were used extensively during WWI & WWII to assist the military and persuade all Americans to help with the war effort.

Using stark imagery to elicit powerful emotions, the posters appealed to people's conscience, fears and ideals of freedom and democracy. The posters called upon every man, woman, and child to make personal sacrifices or adjustments to further the greater national cause. Used for the purposes of recruitment, boosting production, motivation, rationing, conservation, security and financing the War, the posters linked the home front with the military front.

An integral part of wartime communications, the coordination and production of War Posters required considerable resources. To assist, the government enlisted the help of the nation's foremost artists, intellectuals and advertising specialists of the time. Containing uniquely creative and beautiful artwork, War Posters make a great display and are a wonderful reminder of our nation's history.

When the United States entered World War I in April 1917, the Federal Government was faced with the monumental task of mobilizing American society.

Early in the war, President Woodrow Wilson appointed a Committee on Public Information headed by journalist George Creel to lead the propaganda effort.

One way for the Government to get out its message was the poster.

Noted artists volunteered their time and talents to the committee and designed posters urging enlistment in the armed forces, conservation, industrial mobilization, subscriptions to Liberty Loans, and other patriotic duties.

Paul Stahr's design for "Be Patriotic" is typical of many World War I posters. It aimed to be spiritually uplifting and depicted the ideals for which Americans were fighting.

The illustration shown here was used by the US Food Administration to encourage the conservative use of food during World War I.

The Diversity Visa Lottery

At the base of the Statue of Liberty in New York harbor is a poem by Emma Lazarus, "The New Colossus."

> *Not like the brazen giant of Greek fame,*
> *With conquering limbs astride from land to land;*
> *Here at our sea-washed, sunset gates shall stand*
> *A mighty woman with a torch, whose flame*
> *Is the imprisoned lightening, and her name*
> *Mother of Exiles...*
> *"Keep, ancient lands, your storied pomp!" cries she*
> *With silent lips. "Give me your tired, your poor,*
> *Your huddled masses yearning to breathe free.*
> *The wretched refuse of your teeming shore.*
> *Send these the homeless, tempest-tost to me,*
> *I lift my lamp beside the golden door!"*

Lazarus' poem is a message to all potential immigrants as well as a statement of American philosophy.

By placing this message on the base of America's most recognizable symbol Americans supposedly establish what the immigration policy should be. America is a nation founded by and for immigrants. Everyone in America, with the exception of native Americans, are immigrants.

This being the case one would think that we have, or should, live up to the ideals in the poem. Yet America has not always had an open immigration policy. In fact it has often been restrictive.

Introduction

Did you ever hear the Neil Diamond song "America"?

Did you know that Neil Diamond wrote the song "America" in tribute to the impact of immigration in America, it's a song whose lyrics I still remember quite well despite not having heard the song played for probably the best part of twenty years.

The song speaks of the quest for opportunity that embodied million who crossed into this country. Since you are reading this book, you are either considering or have entered the United States Diversity Visa lottery and are hoping to have that opportunity too.

This small volume is by no means definitive, it annals some background to the Diversity Visa program as well as some tips and tricks that you should be aware of when making your application and following up a win with an interview and getting all your documentation and affairs in order.

Unlike many of the other publications you will find on the market I speak about the Diversity Visa Lottery with first hand experience, I won the lottery through my wife and then I won it in my own right the following year. Unlike documents written by attorneys and consultants I can attest to the fact that the lottery system exists and works.

I hope you will find my thoughts and advice useful in your quest to come to America.

Diversity Visa (DV) Overview

I like to think of the Diversity Visa Lottery as something akin to the Ellis Island immigration program. Today visitors to Ellis Island are encumbered only be tourist paraphernalia and not by bundled possessions and the harrowing memory of a transatlantic journey. You're able to retrace the steps of twelve million immigrants who approached America's "front doors to freedom" in the early twentieth century.

Arriving by ferry just like hundreds of thousands of new arrivals between 1897 and 1938, in place of the business-like machinery of immigration inspection, the restored Main Hall now houses the Ellis Island Immigration Museum, dedicated to commemorating the immigrants' stories of trepidation and triumph, courage and rejection, and the lasting image of the American dream.

During its peak years-1892 to 1924 Ellis Island received thousands of immigrants a day. Each was scrutinized for disease or disability as the long line of hopeful new arrivals made their way up the steep stairs to the great, echoing Registry Room. Over 100 million Americans can trace their ancestry in the United States to a man, woman, or child whose name passed from a steamship manifest sheet to an inspector's record book in the great Registry Room at Ellis Island.

With restrictions on immigration in the 1920s Ellis Island's population dwindled, and the station finally closed its doors in 1954. Its grand brick and limestone buildings gradually deteriorated in the fierce weather of New York Harbor.

Concern about this vital part of America's immigrant history led to the inclusion of Ellis Island as part of Statue of Liberty National Monument in 1965.

Private citizens mounted a campaign to preserve the Island, and one of the most ambitious restoration projects in American history returned Ellis Island's Main Building to its former grandeur in September, 1990.

Those days are gone, a glimmer in the colorful past of American Immigration History, today your Visa application is largely automated but that's only the beginning, this small volume will be of some assistance in guiding you through the process of applying, getting your documentation in order and achieving your objective — permanent residence in the United States of America.

To My Parents And Their Unconditional Love And Support.

Immigration and the United States

Immigration has played an important role in American history, and the United States continues to have one of the most open immigration policies in the world despite the attacks of September 11.

Before the era of rapid communications and transportation, America encouraged relatively open immigration to settle its empty lands. After certain states passed immigration laws following the Civil War, the Supreme Court in 1875 declared the regulation of immigration a federal responsibility.

The Immigration Service was established in 1891 to deal with the big increase in immigration which started in 1880.

The outbreak of World War I reduced immigration from Europe, but mass immigration resumed upon the war's conclusion, and Congress responded with a new immigration policy: the national-origins quota system passed in 1921 and revised in 1924.

Immigration was limited at that time by assigning each nationality a quota based on its representation in past U.S. census figures. In 1924, Congress created the U.S. Border Patrol within the Immigration Service and thus a federal police force for the nation's borders and ports.

There was very little immigration during the late 1920's and 1930's, with net immigration actually dropping below zero for several years during the Depression. Immigration remained relatively low during the 20 years following World War II, because the 1920s national-origins system remained in place after Congress re-codified and combined all previous immigration and naturalization law into the Immigration and Nationality Act of 1952. American agriculture continued to import seasonal labor from Mexico, as they had during the war, under a 1951 formal agreement between the United States and Mexico that made the Bracero Program permanent.

In 1965, Congress replaced the national origins system with a preference system designed to unite immigrant families and attract skilled immigrants to the United States. This change to national policy responded to changes in the sources of immigration since 1924.

The majority of applicants for immigration visas now came from Asia and Latin America rather than Europe.

The preference system continued to limit the number of immigration visas available each year, however, and Congress still responded to refugees with special legislation. It was not until the Refugee Act of 1980 that the United States had a general policy governing the admission of refugees. Depending on where you live in the world, you may be eligible for a residence Visa as a refugee.

The DV Program

In 1995, Congress established a Diversity Visa Program that authorized up to 50,000 immigrant visas annually to persons from countries that were underrepresented among the 400,000 to 500,000 immigrants coming to the United States each year.

Most immigration to the United States is based upon family relationships or employment. Diversity visa applicants, however, can qualify on the basis of education and/or work experience.

Applicants need only to demonstrate that they have the equivalent of a U.S. high school education or two years of work experience in an occupation that requires at least two years of training or experience.

If ultimately selected as lottery winners, like other immigrant applicants, they are subject to all of the grounds upon which a visa can be denied, including medical condition and criminal behavior.

The Diversity Visa lottery was established to ensure diversity in the immigrant population of the United States.

Full-scope diversity—this is why citizens from countries like India, China and England, from which many people have already migrated to the U.S., are no longer eligible to enter the diversity lottery. The Diversity Visa Lottery program was designed to offer equitable opportunities around the world for people of diverse nationalities to live in the United States.

Recently, some lawmakers voted to put an end to the

green card lottery, but the results of this movement remain to be seen.

Originally, the Diversity Visa Program was one of many immigrant visa functions assigned to the National Visa Center at Portsmouth, New Hampshire.

In September 2000, diversity visa processing was moved to a newly remodeled site at Williamsburg, Kentucky, the Kentucky Consular Center (KCC).

Unlike earlier lottery programs, KCC processes lottery applications in the United States, thereby relieving overseas missions of many clerical and file storage responsibilities. Kentucky Consular Center employees receive and process lottery entries, select winners, process winners' visa applications, and schedule applicant interviews at missions abroad.

Consular officers at the missions issue or deny the applications.

The KCC has an impressive ability to eliminate duplicate entries based on addresses and names electronically, including the use of facial recognition technology. New technologies can do the many procedures that simply were not possible when seven million or fifteen million envelopes came in by hand.

Until 2003, the diversity visa lottery was paper-based, which the Department characterized as labor intensive, inefficient, and costly. However, the Department implemented an entirely electronic registration system called E-DV for the DV-2005 lottery, which received nearly six million entries via the Internet during the two-month registration period.

At the time of writing the second E-DV round had just closed and winners were being notified to start the visa application process. Using facial and name recognition technology and data mining techniques, each winner will be checked against the database of all other applicants to identify duplicate entries, which will result in disqualification.

The Department believes once E-DV is further implemented, these types of fraud will be less likely to occur.

The current diversity visa processing fee is collected only from applicants selected as winners. Millions of applicants, therefore, pay nothing to participate, and the U.S. government pays all costs not covered by the diversity visa fee.

For fiscal 2002, the Department estimated that program costs not covered by the fee exceeded $840,000. It has been recommended that the State Department collect processing fees from all persons who apply for the diversity visa program, and in addition, it has been determined that no current diversity visa fees are allotted to fraud prevention. Antifraud activities at post are generally dominated by nonimmigrant visa fraud cases. Many embassies and consulates with significant diversity visa issues, therefore, do not routinely refer problem cases to their antifraud units, and some missions have no antifraud units. As a result it has been recommended that the State Department determine whether antifraud field investigations are useful in diversity visa cases and how the diversity visa fee could be appropriately devoted to antifraud work at overseas missions.

The Department charges nothing for entry into the program and has determined that charging a small fee for the paper-based registration system is impractical.

Although for paper-based applications it may not be feasible, the new electronic system may open the door for charging a fee that will cover program costs and the associated administrative costs. According to a sample taken from one region of applicants, about 50 percent of applicants apply from the United States and 70 percent of applicants already use a facilitator to assist with registration.

Many of these facilitators can be found on the Internet and charge fees for services. Using an electronic payment system, applicants could pay a small fee for diversity visa registration, enabling the U.S. government to recoup costs and fund more fraud prevention officers overseas, especially in countries with critical fraud problems.

Such an approach might also reduce multiple entries since applications would no longer be free.

Legal immigration alone in the 1990s likely matched or exceeded the previous historical peak decade of 1901-1910, when 8.8 million legal immigrants were admitted.

Adding the settlement of illegal aliens makes the 1990s without doubt the period of greatest immigration in America's history.

Entering the Diversity Visa Lottery

Each year, the Diversity Lottery (DV) Program makes 55,000 immigrant visas available through a lottery to people who come from countries with low rates of immigration to the United States.

Since 1999, 5,000 are allocated for use under the Nicaraguan and Central American Relief Act (NACARA). The State Department holds the lottery every year, and randomly selects approximately 110,000 applicants from all qualified entries. The State Department selects the approximately 110,000 applications since many will not complete the visa process.

However once 55,000 are issued or the fiscal year ends, the Diversity Visa program is closed.

If you receive a visa through the Diversity Visa Lottery Program you will be authorized to live and work permanently in the United States.

You will also be allowed to bring your spouse and any unmarried children under the age of 21 to the United States.

The lists below show the countries whose natives are qualified within each geographic region for the diversity program.

The determination of countries within each region is based on information provided by the Geographer of the Department of State and varies from year to year.

The countries whose natives do not qualify for the

Diversity Visa program are identified by the Bureau of Citizenship and Immigration Services (BCIS) according to the formula in Section 203(c) of the Immigration and Nationality Act.

Dependent areas overseas are included within the region of the governing country.

The countries whose natives do not qualify for this diversity program (because they are the principal source countries of Family-Sponsored and Employment-Based immigration or "high admission" countries) are noted in parentheses after the respective regional lists

AFRICA

Algeria, Angola, Benin, Botswana, Burkina Faso, Burundi, Cameroon, Cape Verde, Central African Republic, Chad, Comoros, Congo, Congo, Democratic Republic of the

Cote D'Ivoire (Ivory Coast), Djibouti, Egypt, Equatorial Guinea, Eritrea, Ethiopia, Gabon

Gambia, The Ghana, Guinea, Guinea-Bissau, Kenya, Lesotho, Liberia, Libya, Madagascar, Malawi, Mali, Mauritania, Mauritius, Morocco, Mozambique,

Namibia, Niger, Nigeria, Rwanda, Sao Tome and Principe, Senegal, Seychelles, Sierra Leone, Somalia, South Africa, Sudan, Swaziland, Tanzania, Togo, Tunisia, Uganda, Zambia, Zimbabwe

ASIA

Afghanistan, Bahrain, Bangladesh, Bhutan, Brunei, Burma, Cambodia, East Timor, Hong Kong Special Administrative Region, Indonesia, Iran, Iraq, Israel, Japan, Jordan, Kuwait, Laos, Lebanon, Malaysia, Maldives, Mongolia, Nepal, North Korea, Oman, Qatar, Saudi Arabia, Singapore, Sri Lanka, Syria, Taiwan, Thailand, United Arab Emirates, Yemen

Natives of the following Asian countries do not qualify for this year's diversity program: China [mainland-born], India, Pakistan, South Korea, Philippines, and Vietnam.

The Hong Kong S.A.R and Taiwan do qualify and are listed above. Macau S.A.R. also qualifies.

EUROPE

Albania, Andorra, Armenia, Austria, Azerbaijan, Belarus, Belgium, Bosnia and Herzegovina, Bulgaria, Croatia, Cyprus, Czech Republic, Denmark (including components and dependent areas overseas), Estonia, Finland, France (including components and dependent areas overseas), Georgia, Germany, Greece, Hungary, Iceland, Ireland, Italy, Kazakhstan, Kyrgyzstan, Latvia , Liechtenstein, Lithuania, Luxembourg, Macau Special Administrative Region, Macedonia, the Former Yugoslav Republic, Malta, Moldova, Monaco, Netherlands (including components and dependent areas overseas), Northern Ireland, Norway, Poland, Portugal (including components and dependent areas overseas), Romania, San Marino, Serbia and Montenegro, Slovakia, Slovenia, Spain, Sweden, Switzerland, Tajikistan, Turkey, Turkmenistan, Ukraine, Uzbekistan, Vatican City

Natives of the following European countries do not qualify for this year's diversity program: Great Britain and Russia. Great Britain (United Kingdom) includes the following dependent areas: Anguilla, Bermuda, British Virgin Islands, Cayman Islands, Falkland Islands, Gibraltar, Montserrat, Pitcairn, St. Helena, Turks and Caicos Islands.

Note that for purposes of the diversity program only, Northern Ireland is treated separately; Northern Ireland does qualify and is listed among the qualifying areas.

NORTH AMERICA

The Bahamas

In North America, natives of Canada and Mexico do not qualify for the diversity program.

OCEANIA

Australia (including components and dependent areas overseas), Fiji, Kiribati

Marshall Islands, Micronesia, Federated States of, Nauru, New Zealand (including components and dependent areas overseas)Palau, Papua New Guinea, Solomon Islands

Tonga, Tuvalu, Vanuatu, Samoa

SOUTH AMERICA, CENTRAL AMERICA, AND THE CARIBBEAN

Antigua and Barbuda, Argentina, Barbados, Belize, Bolivia, Brazil, Chile, Costa Rica, Cuba, Dominica, Ecuador, Grenada, Guatemala, Guyana, Honduras, Nicaragua, Panama, Paraguay, Peru, Saint Kitts and Nevis, Saint Lucia, Saint Vincent and the Grenadines, Suriname, Trinidad and Tobago, Uruguay, Venezuela

Countries in this region whose natives do not qualify for this year's diversity program: Colombia, Dominican Republic, El Salvador, Haiti, Jamaica, and Mexico.

Starting in 2003, entries to the Diversity Visa lottery must be submitted online at www.dvlottery.state.gov. (This site is only accessible during the application period.)

Paper entries or mail-in requests will no longer be accepted.

Lottery entrants must include a passport-style digital photograph and separate digital photographs of any spouse and children under 21 years of age.

Group or family photographs are not allowed.

Be aware also, that you may submit only one entry during any particular Diversity Visa lottery; those who submit more than one entry will be disqualified.

Spouses may submit separate entries if they meet the eligibility requirements.

If only one spouse is selected, the other may enter the country on the Diversity Visa of the winning spouse.

Basically the Diversity Visa lottery has two eligibility requirements:

Entrants must have been born in an eligible country, or have parents who were born in eligible countries and who were not residents of the country of birth, when the entrant was born. For example, parents might have lived temporarily in the ineligible country because of their jobs. Every year, the State Department announces the countries whose natives are ineligible for application.

Entrants must meet an education or training requirement. If you have a high school education or have successfully completed a 12-year course of elementary and secondary education you will have met the training requirement.

If you have at least two years of work experience within the past five years in an occupation requiring at least two years of training or experience to perform then you will have also met the education or training requirement. For a list of qualifying occupations, visit http://travel.state.gov/

You'll need to answer a few questions and provide passport-style digital photographs through upload.

The general instructions are deceptively simple and whilst you are no longer required to submit paper versions of the applications, you need to be aware that the State Department is very wary of fraud and thus demands strict compliance with the rules and instructions for entry.

A minor typographical error appears to raise a presumption of fraud to the State Department because it has concluded that most errors, particularly in the spelling of the name, indicate that duplicate petitions may have been filed.

Any differences in the spelling of a name on the petition when compared to the birth certificate will disqualify the applicant outright.

Almost three million applications were disqualified from the DV-2004 program for failure to comply with the instructions to the letter.

Submit only one entry. If you submit more than one, you will be disqualified.

Selection of entries is randomly done by computer.

Spouses who are eligible for the Diversity Visa lottery can apply separately; the "losing" spouse can enter the country on the Diversity Visa of the "winning" spouse.

This is the only legitimate way to significantly increase your chance of entering the U.S. through the Diversity Visa lottery.

You'll get an acknowledgment from the State Department once you've submitted your entry.

The State Department awards visas to winners on a first-come, first-served basis and in addition, a winning application is only valid for one federal fiscal year (October 1 — September 30)

Do I qualify to enter?

You *may* qualify to enter if:

YOU were BORN in one of the Lottery countries; OR YOUR HUSBAND OR WIFE was BORN in a Lottery country; OR In some circumstances, YOUR MOTHER OR FATHER was BORN in a Lottery country, (Please check the eligible and ineligible countries list)

and:

YOU have a high school diploma; OR The equivalent of a high school diploma; OR Two or more years of work experience in an occupation which requires at least two years of training or experience.

How about my family?

If you receive a green card through the DV Program, your spouse and unmarried children under 21 years old will also be simultaneously entitled to green cards, unless they have independent problems.

The spouse or child does not have to be born in one of the qualifying countries.

All children over 21 years of age must file separate applications.

Facilitators and Fraudsters

The Federal Trade Commission Bureau of Consumer Protection Office of Consumer and Business Education (FTC) recently issued a consumer alert regarding websites and companies purporting to offered 'guaranteed' ways for people to win the Diversity Visa Lottery

Hiring a company or attorney to enter the lottery for you is your decision, but the person you pay will have to follow the same procedure described earlier. And your chance of being selected is the same whether you submit the entry or you pay someone to do it for you.

If you or someone you know is trying to get a green card and thus the right to live in the United States permanently you need to be on the lookout for unscrupulous businesses and attorneys.

For a fee, fraudsters claim that they can make it easier to enter the State Department's annual Diversity Visa lottery or at least increase your chances of winning the Diversity Visa lottery.

At present there are of course no fees to enter the lottery.

Some businesses and attorneys misrepresent their services by saying that:• they are affiliated with the U.S. government;• state that they have special expertise or a special entry form that is required to enter the lottery.

Such companies may make claims that they have never

had a lottery entry rejected; that they can increase an entrant's chances of "winning" the lottery

More importantly, they may make claims that people from ineligible countries still are "qualified" to enter the lottery.

Such companies may jeopardize an entrant's opportunity to participate in the lottery by filing several entries. These companies also may charge lottery-winning applicants substantial fees to complete the application process.

A delay in processing a winner's application can ruin their chance for a green card because of the 2-1 selection process (110,000 winners are notified although only the first 55,000 will get visas)

Be skeptical of Web sites posing as U.S. government sites. They may have domain names similar to government agencies, official-looking emblems (eagles, flags, or other American images like the Statue of Liberty or the U.S. Capitol), the official seals or logos of and links to government sites, and list Washington, D.C., mailing addresses. If the domain name doesn't end in ".gov," it's not a government site.

Fraudulent sites may charge you for government forms. Don't pay; government forms and instructions for completing them are available from the issuing U.S. government agency for free.

Remember, there's no charge to enter the green card lottery. You can enter on your own at the State Department's Web site—www.dvlottery.state.gov.

Visas, caveats and Documentation

There are a number of visas available from tourist visas to student visas and special occupation visas. A visit to your local United States of America embassy or a check on the State Department web site will assist you in determining what visas may be available to you.

As a holder of another type of visa, like one of those described above, you are still able to apply for a Diversity Visa.

If you enter the Diversity Visa program and are unsuccessful you should nonetheless be aware that the State Department has held that a lottery application is, an expression of interest in immigrating to the United States, the entry is a "petition" within the terms of the Immigration and Naturalisation Act (INA) and you should disclose lottery participation on any other visa applications, which request information as to whether an immigrant visa petition has been submitted and that this information may result in a visa denial pursuant to the Act.

Many people view the lottery application as a simple matter not worthy of disclosure in another application. Given the stakes, certain persons may not wish to risk applying for a lottery, in which only a small chance of winning is weighed against the necessity of obtaining student visas necessary to complete a program, particularly if travel or an extension of stay is required.

Many "winners" who lost the race will now experience difficulty obtaining student and visitor nonimmigrant visas and may not even be able to enter the United States. Having made advanced efforts to become a permanent resident, they have expressed clear immigrant intent and may not be able overcome INA §214(b), which requires unrelinquished domicile abroad.

For example, an F-1 student from the middle east who chose to consular process in a country other than his country of birth, may now be unable to obtain a F-1 student visa to return the United States to resume his studies. This same problem arises for applicants who were unable to adjust status before September 30, 2003. Such individuals are placed in removal proceedings if they failed to maintain underlying lawful nonimmigrant status.

Diversity visa participants should also be aware that the State Department no longer shreds unused and/or unselected diversity lottery applications.

On September 12, 2002, Representative George Gekas, Chairman of the House Judiciary Committee's Subcommittee on Immigration, Border Security and Claims, announced that upon his suggestion, the ten to thirteen million diversity visa applications will be shared with U.S. law enforcement and intelligence agencies.

The diversity visa program, which had once given hope to vast hordes of wishful immigrants both in the United States and abroad, may now become a security trap. Having the name, date and country of birth and address of the ten to thirteen million applicants would hardly appear useful to

intelligence agencies, but may be useful to an agency searching for current addresses of the several hundred thousand people ordered removed or who have overstayed their visas.

After fifteen years of visa lotteries, the present government's attitude towards immigrants has made it necessary to recommend caution to persons entering the diversity visa lottery who may be out of status or otherwise removable.

Finally, be alert to Web sites and advertisements promising government travel or residency documents online or by mail.

Except for entering the Diversity Visa lottery, most applications for visas, passports, green cards, and other travel and residency documents must be completed in person before an officer of the U.S. government.

Take care about who you send your personal documents to.

Unless you have established relationships with businesses, do not mail birth certificates, passports, drivers' licenses, marriage certificates, National Identification or Social Security cards, or other documents with your personal identifying information to businesses promising to complete your application for travel or residency documents.

These businesses may be engaged in identity theft.

You've entered — now what?

Entry into the Diversity Visa program is never a 'sure thing' certainly people from slightly less common countries like Botswana, New Zealand and Yemen have a better chance.

Each of the eligible countries is assigned to one of the six geographic regions previously described.

An annual limit is determined for each of the 6 regions using a formula based on the preceding five years' immigrant admissions and the region's population total. .

The leading countries of admission vary from year to year. See Appendix 1 for the DV-2005 figures.

Unlike previous years, since the introduction of the online petition, you now are assured of the fact that your entry is in.

When I entered the lottery a couple of years ago I entered from a foreign country by post. Although my wife was not born in an eligible country, because she was married to me, I was able to get her to enter a petition also.

It was only in February of the following year that we heard that my wife had won the lottery.

The announcement came as a letter by post of congratulations accompanied by a wad of forms classified as a "Packet Three" to be completed and returned as soon as possible to the KCC.

Getting Your House in Order

Winners who choose to immigrant visa process can file their properly completed "Packet Three" with the KCC before October 1st, the beginning of the fiscal year and should try to do so as soon as possible.

When their rank-order or case number becomes current, the National Visa Center will send the winner the "Packet Four", which includes the appointment notices for visa interviews at the U.S. consular posts

Remember that getting the letter of congratulations is only the first step of several. You have a number of additional matters to address before you can be sure that you have a Diversity Visa.

The revelation that we were winners was somewhat surprising, I never knew anyone who had ever one a Diversity Visa and when I looked on the internet I quickly found that it was not an uncommon occurrence. Since I moved to America I have met many people from all walks of life who have won the Diversity Visa Lottery.

The Application— Packet Three

Follow the instruction sheet in "Packet Three" from the KCC to the letter; this usually accompanies all the forms and the congratulatory letter.

Top of the list for us was completion of the relevant forms as soon as possible, and their return. You can return these forms by the most expedient method available. We mailed them, however you could send them by registered mail or by courier like DHL

One of the most important things that we discovered was that the forms must be completed fully. You must not leave anything blank.

Because we didn't actually know anyone in America we were not in a position to state where we were going to live, so we left this space blank. We very soon found out that this was unacceptable and our forms were returned some weeks later as incomplete.

Even if you do not know where you are going to live, you should indicate UNKNOWN.

By the time you are ready for your consular or mission interview though, you should have determined where you plan to move to and you should have an address and a name that your green card can be sent to once you make your first entry into the US.

If you don't know anyone in the United States, try to establish a relationship with a financial institution, a bank or a church or social community.

You may even want to consider making a tourist visit to the United States and establishing a postal mail box with one of the 3rd party mailbox operators like PostNet or a UPS store, found in most suburban shopping areas or city centers.

Usually these places will sell you a mailbox rental for periods of up to a year upon supply of a copy of your passport or some valid form of identification and some sort of address—we started by using the guest house address that we were staying with and then changed this when we moved into more permanent accommodation.

In parallel with completion of the forms you should ensure that you have all your other documentation in order, many of these things seem very simple, ordinary and even mundane until you have to physically make the effort to get them

You will be required to take along a number of ¾ colour passport photographs to the interview, which will accompany all the other documentation that you will submit under "Packet Four".

Identification Papers

Second on the list was getting originals or all our birth certificates with full names, indicating the names and dates of birth of our parents and those of our children.

Ensure that your passports are valid for at least a further six months.

Ordinarily you would have these; however passports are often overlooked by people particularly if they do not travel frequently and if they are in a foreign language, some people have never even had a passport before and may discover that this takes time to request.

You may need to get a certified translation of your identification documents into English.

Police Clearance

Third on the list of required documents was a set of Police Clearance certificates for every country we had lived in for more than six months since we turned the age of 16.

Under normal circumstances this would not be a problem for most people; however we have lived in several countries since we were sixteen years of age, and thus we had to go through a very complicated procedure of getting certificates from all the countries we had lived in. Failure to do this could jeopardize your petition.

You needn't worry about parking violations and not criminal misdemeanors however all serious offenses that may be recorded against you in your police record can count against you in qualifying.

The Police Clearance certificate is usually based on a finger print search in the national database of each respective country where you have lived.

If you have some sort of criminal record, your petition may be refused.

If the Police Clearance is in a foreign language you may need to get it translated.

Qualifications

Proof of Education is next on your list, you should be able to produce evidence of education, these should come in the form of:

- school leaving certificate
- university degrees
- diplomas
- certifications

Include any other form of educational documentation that you might have with your interview documents.

If you cannot provide evidence of schooling or occupational training your petition may be refused.

You may also be required to get accreditations of your academic qualifications, these are fairly straightforward to obtain but in the end are not as useful as they represent, particularly when trying to obtain professional certifications etc.

Chartered Accountants for example have to be certificated members of either the Canadian or Australian Accounting Associations in order to receive equivalent recognition in the United States. Most other qualified Chartered Accountants have to requalify.

Most technology qualifications are recognized because they have their origins in international associations and certification programs.

Your University qualifications may require an equivalency assessment.

If your certifications are in a foreign language you may need to get them translated

Finances — Public Charge

The final piece of the information pile is evidence of your ability to be self sufficient and evidence that you are unlikely to become a burden on the social security system.

This is a bit of a grey area in terms of what exactly is required.

Essentially, in our case we formulated a balance sheet of our assets and provided six months worth of financial statements to demonstrate our ability to generate an income.

In addition we provided letters of reference from our previous employers indicating our professionalism and employability.

If you have an employer lined up in the US even though you do not have a visa, this will also help in your petition. You will need to get the prospective employer to provide a letter of guaranteed offer of employment.

Essentially, you must meet the public charge category by showing that you are self-supporting, have sufficient skills and/or education to find employment, or have friends or family who will support you on arrival in the United States. With 2004 Poverty Income Guidelines at $23,562 for a family of four, you have quite a high standard to meet.

In many countries only a small percentage of the population earns over $23,562 annually.

For example, Bangladesh, which had 5,126 registrants

for DV-2004 program, has a GDP capita income of only \$1,610 and an adult literacy rate of 59.4 percent. Accordingly, only the wealthiest sector of Bangladeshi society can overcome INA §212(a)(4), which states that *"a person who, in the opinion of the consular or immigration official, is likely to become a public charge"* is excludable.

As in any immigrant visa application, you must show sufficient assets, income or a sponsorship to meet the poverty guidelines.

Since many DV winners have no pre-arranged employment or family ties in the United States, this issue arises frequently.

The Interview

Once you have submitted the forms to the KCC you will have to simply wait until they send you notification that you are scheduled for an interview with a specific embassy or consular mission.

Some people pick embassies or missions in particular parts of the world that will suit their particular circumstance.

By example, we chose the mission that was closest to where we were living at the time in Riyadh, the capital of Saudi Arabia.

We could have just as easily chosen the United States Embassy in London, England; however that would have required us to travel to London for the interview.

In the end, whilst we were interviewed in Saudi Arabia, our teenage daughter who was at college in England, was interviewed at the Embassy in London.

Interviews are conducted according to your rank-number. Accordingly, every couple of months the rank-order increases. You can estimate fairly accurately as to when exactly your interview will take place.

When the time comes for your interview you will receive "Packet Four".

Packet Four requires you to schedule a time with the embassy or consular mission for the interview.

The Embassy will advise you who the designated medical examiner is and will advise you to attend a medical examination and bring the medical certificates with you to the interview. The medical examination usually involves blood and urine tests and x-rays. The objective is to ensure that you have no medical diseases or ailments that might be considered contagious or potentially burdensome to the state. The examiner will usually require you to bring along a full set of inoculation certificates. If you have not been inoculated, you may be inoculated on the spot for certain diseases.

The entire family of prospective immigrants will need to appear before the consular official.

Your interview could be a very quick procedure or a long arduous one depending on where you are having the interview.

The consular official has right of veto over your petition so how you conduct yourself at this interview is critical.

You will need to pay for your visa applications at the time of the interview.

One of the questions that you will most probably be asked will be "Why do you want to live in America"—you will need to think carefully about your answer.

The interview represents different things to different people, for some it is a real test of their nerves. If you have all your documentation in order and you have answered all the questions honestly and you are not disease-ridden you should have no problems.

You will need to provide the consular official with at least copies of all your documentation that you are submitting. It is likely that the consular official will want to keep the police clearance certificates so be sure to make copies of these for your own records.

Have I got the Visa ?

It is very rarely that the visa is granted immediately, usually at this time the consular official will advise you whether or not he plans to take your application further.

The next steps at the mission, will be to undertake a federal criminal or Interpol search. Essentially this is an attempt to ensure that you are not a known felon or criminal.

Assuming you have passed all the other criteria you should be able to get your visa within a month of the interview.

You can now resign your existing job and sell your house !

I got the Visa—now what ?

The visa is valid for six months from the date of issue.

Within six months of issue of the visa you should make your first entry into the US.

When arriving at the Port of Entry, you will all need to be in attendance or at very least the two parents under whom the chargeability was determined.

In my case, my wife would not have been able to enter if I was not in attendance since she would not have been Diversity Visa eligible if I was not about.

The immigration official will likely pose some questions to you and will ask you for the packet four that would have been given to you at the time that you were issued the visa.

The official will not return this packet but will instead enter a temporary visa into your passport.

This packet of documents enters the visa processing system and will result in the issue of a green card to you. This is sent to you by mail and is usually valid for ten years and which will be sent to the address that you indicated in Packet Three. Every renewal time you will need to pay for the renewal.

When you now enter and exit the US you will be required to present your green card and your passport.

Well done, you are now a permanent resident and Green card holder.

After five years of contiguous residence you can apply for US citizenship.

Social Security Number

Amongst the Packet Three documents is an application form for a Social Security Number (SSN).

Theoretically a Social Security Number will be generated for you and the necessary documentation will be sent to the same address as your green card when you hand in the envelope to the immigration official.

This doesn't always happen—you may need to pay a visit to your local Social Security Administration Office.

Your next steps are to commence establishing a credit history and this can only be successfully achieved using your Social Security Number. You will need your SSN when applying for your bank account, credit cards or when registering to take a driver's licence.

Your SSN becomes the key to who you are in the system.

Appendix 1

Diversity Visa Lottery 2005 (DV-2005) Results

The Kentucky Consular Center in Williamsburg, Kentucky, has registered and notified the winners of the DV-2005 diversity lottery. The diversity lottery was conducted under the terms of section 203(c) of the Immigration and Nationality Act and makes available *50,000 permanent resident visas annually to persons from countries with low rates of immigration to the United States. Approximately 100,000 applicants have been registered and notified and may now make an application for an immigrant visa. Since it is likely that some of the first *50,000 persons registered will not pursue their cases to visa issuance, this larger figure should insure that all DV-2005 numbers will be used during fiscal year 2005 (October 1, 2004 until September 30, 2005).

Applicants registered for the DV-2005 program were selected at random from more than 9.5 million qualified entries received during the 60-day application period that ran from 12:00 AM on November 1, 2003, until midnight, December 30, 2003. The visas have been apportioned among six geographic regions, with a maximum of seven percent available to persons born in any single country. During the visa interview, principal applicants must provide proof of a high school education or its equivalent, or show two years of work experience in an occupation that requires at least two years of training or experience within the past five years. Those selected will need to act on their immigrant visa applications quickly. Applicants should follow the instructions in their notification letter and must fully complete the information requested.

Registrants living legally in the United States who wish to apply for adjustment of their status must contact the Bureau of Citizenship and Immigration Services for information on the requirements and procedures. Once the total *50,000 visa numbers have been used, the program for fiscal year 2005 will end. Selected applicants who do not receive visas by September 30, 2005 will derive no further benefit from their DV-2005 registration. Similarly, spouses and children accompanying or following to join DV-2005 principal applicants are entitled to derivative diversity visa status only until September 30, 2005.

Only participants in the DV-2005 program who were selected for further processing have been notified. Those who have not received notification were not selected. They may try for the upcoming DV-2006 lottery if they wish. The dates for the registration period for the DV-2006 lottery program will be widely publicized during August 2004.

* The Nicaraguan and Central American Relief Act (NACARA) passed by Congress in November 1997 stipulated that up to 5,000 of the 55,000 annually-allocated diversity visas be made available for use under the NACARA program. The reduction of the limit of available visas to 50,000 began with DV-2000.

The following is the statistical breakdown by foreign-state chargeability of those registered for the DV-2005 program:

AFRICA

ALGERIA 1,489
ANGOLA 14
BENIN 233
BOTSWANA 7
BURKINA FASO 76
BURUNDI 34
CAMEROON 1,540
CAPE VERDE 6
CENTRAL AFRICAN REP. 4
CHAD 22
COMOROS 3
CONGO 47
CONGO, DEMOCRATIC
REPUBLIC OF THE 844
COTE D'IVOIRE 321
DJIBOUTI 12
EGYPT 6,070
EQUATORIAL GUINEA 2
ERITREA 556
ETHIOPIA 6,060
GABON 29
GAMBIA, THE 136
GHANA 3,974
GUINEA 268
GUINEA-BISSAU 3
KENYA 3,618
LESOTHO 0
LIBERIA 714

LIBYA 35
MADAGASCAR 28
MALAWI 44
MALI 124
MAURITANIA 25
MAURITIUS 23
MOROCCO 5,298
MOZAMBIQUE 12
NAMIBIA 11
NIGER 53
NIGERIA 6,725
RWANDA 51
SAO TOME AND PRINCIPE 0
SENEGAL 409
SEYCHELLES 4
SIERRA LEONE 594
SOMALIA 364
SOUTH AFRICA 390
SUDAN 1,015
SWAZILAND 6
TANZANIA 356
TOGO 2,857
TUNISIA 134
UGANDA 244
ZAMBIA 118
ZIMBABWE 141

ASIA

AFGHANISTAN 22
BAHRAIN 1
BANGLADESH 7,404
BHUTAN 1
BRUNEI 1
BURMA 531
CAMBODIA 164
HONG KONG SP. ADMIN. REGION 77
INDONESIA 258
IRAN 820
IRAQ 48
ISRAEL 116
JAPAN 373
JORDAN 44
NORTH KOREA 1
KUWAIT 16
LAOS 4
LEBANON 83
MALAYSIA 87
MALDIVES 0
MONGOLIA 55
NEPAL 2,698
OMAN 0
QATAR 1
SAUDI ARABIA 30
SINGAPORE 35
SRI LANKA 386
SYRIA 26

THAILAND 102
TAIWAN 367
UNITED ARAB EMIRATES 13
YEMEN 40

EUROPE

ALBANIA 3,380
ANDORRA 1
ARMENIA 1,004
AUSTRIA 91
AZERBAIJAN 235
BELARUS 925
BELGIUM 81
BOSNIA & HERZEGOVINA 103
BULGARIA 4,068
CROATIA 69
CYPRUS 14
CZECH REPUBLIC 169
DENMARK 42
ESTONIA 64
FINLAND 59
FRANCE 384
French Southern & Antarctic Lands 1
Martinique 2
New Caledonia 1
Reunion 3
GEORGIA 375
GERMANY 1,275
GREECE 78
HUNGARY 181
ICELAND 5
IRELAND 205
ITALY 202
KAZAKHSTAN 296

KYRGYZSTAN 206
LATVIA 158
LIECHTENSTEIN 1
LITHUANIA 1,114
LUXEMBOURG 2
MACEDONIA, FORMER YUGOSLAV REP. OF 306
MALTA 0
MOLDOVA 383
MONACO 0
NETHERLANDS 130
Netherlands Antilles 10
Aruba 2
NORTHERN IRELAND 75
NORWAY 25
POLAND 6,211
PORTUGAL 51
Macau 12
ROMANIA 2,521
SAN MARINO 0
SERBIA & MONTENEGRO 425
SLOVAKIA 398
SLOVENIA 6
SPAIN 134
SWEDEN 115
SWITZERLAND 136
TAJIKISTAN 83
TURKEY 1,803
TURKMENISTAN 78
UKRAINE 5,361
UZBEKISTAN 1,551
VATICAN CITY 0

NORTH AMERICA

OCEANIA

AUSTRALIA 787
Cocos Islands 2
FIJI 530
KIRIBATI 0
MARSHALL ISLANDS 0
MICRONESIA, FEDERATED STATES OF 0
NAURU 0
NEW ZEALAND 290
Cook Islands 0
Niue 1
PALAU 2
PAPUA NEW GUINEA 5
SAMOA 6
SOLOMON ISLANDS 1
TONGA 96
TUVALU 0
VANUATU 0

SOUTH AMERICA, CENTRAL AMERICA, AND THE CARIBBEAN

ANTIGUA AND BARBUDA 4
ARGENTINA 221
BARBADOS 12
BELIZE 3
BOLIVIA 108
BRAZIL 592
CHILE 43
COSTA RICA 24
CUBA 674
DOMINICA 8
ECUADOR 308
GRENADA 7
GUATEMALA 25
GUYANA 27
HONDURAS 35
NICARAGUA 14
PANAMA 17
PARAGUAY 14
PERU 2,514
SAINT KITTS AND NEVIS 3
SAINT LUCIA 4

SAINT VINCENT AND
THE GRENADINES 14
SURINAME 3
TRINIDAD AND TOBAGO 96
URUGUAY 18
VENEZUELA 299

Natives of the following countries were not eligible to participate in DV-2005: Canada, China (mainland-born, excluding Hong Kong S.A.R., and Taiwan), Colombia, Dominican Republic, El Salvador, Haiti, India, Jamaica, Mexico, Pakistan, the Philippines, Russia, South Korea, United Kingdom (except Northern Ireland) and its dependent territories, and Vietnam.

2004/806

[End]

Released on July 22, 2004

http://www.ftc.gov/bcp/conline/pubs/alerts/lottery.htm

http://www.travel.state.gov/dv2005.html

http://www.travel.state.gov/visa/dv-06_bulletin.pdf